W9-ARN-409

LIVING TO L.E.A.D.

A Story of PASSION, PURPOSE and GRIT

CJ STEWART

PUBLISHING

CONNECT·INSPIRE·INFLUENCE

Copyright © 2017

All rights reserved. No part of this book may be reproduced, stored in a retrieval system, or transmitted in any form or by any means, electronic, mechanical, photocopying, recording, scanning, or otherwise, without the prior written permission of the publisher.

Disclaimer

All the material contained in this book is provided for educational and informational purposes only. No responsibility can be taken for any results or outcomes resulting from the use of this material.

While every attempt has been made to provide information that is both accurate and effective, the author does not assume any responsibility for the accuracy or use/misuse of this information.

Table of Content

PREFACE

When I look back over my life, there are a lot of interactions with people that have helped prepare me to write this book. Like my grandfather, Horace Dunn, who I watched Cubs games with growing up. Or, my mentor T.J. Wilson who took me to get my first private lesson. People like Preston Douglas who was the Chicago Cubs scout that drafted me not once, but twice and Dave Wilder, Cubs scouting director who demanded structure in an environment of high accountability. Some of these folks were in my life for a long time and others for only a short period of time. No matter the length of time, what they had to give me during the time we spent together was transformational and still stays with me today. It's like the doctors and nurses who were on call when I was born. I don't remember who those people are, but what I do know is that they provided me with what I needed, when I needed it. At that time, it was safe passage from my mother's womb into the world, and even though I don't see those folks on a regular basis, it doesn't diminish the profound effect they had on my life during the appointed time that we met.

One of the most life-changing and influential people in my life is a childhood friend named Antwon who we also called Twon. Antwon had charisma, he was a grinder, a hustler and he was his brother's keeper. We were about 11 years old when we met, and although he's older than me by only a year, he handled business like a man. He was my first agent; whatever team he told me to play for, whatever schedule he told me to play, that's what I did. During the summer, I used to go over Antwon's house in Embarcadero in College Park. The block was always hot in Embarcadero and you had to keep your street sense about you at all times, and even though I wasn't from there, I felt safe because of Antwon. When I got dropped off over Twon's house I had no money, just my baseball gear and some clothes. I didn't care about the surroundings at all; I knew that staying with Twon for the summer was the only way I was going to make all of my baseball commitments and that's all that mattered to me. There was a lot of love in his household. If his mom had a spot on the floor for you to catch, then you could stay. Between Twon and his brothers, their apartment was like the Boys and Girls Club; it was so many of us over there.

Even though I had no money when I was there, I ate good all the time and whenever I needed baseball stuff I always had it. As far as I knew, Twon paid my registration fees, too; I had no clue. All I knew is that I was playing baseball and I was having the time of my life. Years later when Twon and I were reminiscing about those times, I learned that he took care of us by hustlin'. Here he was, a kid, putting his life in danger not only for himself, but also looking out for me. He never threw that up to my face or made it a point of contention in our relationship. He was just a true friend, period. Now in no way am I condoning hustlin' (nor does Twon), but what I am saying is sometimes you're dealt a hand in life and without the proper guidance and support, you'll do what you understand the best in order to survive.

As we grew older, we played against each other on a few teams and then we came back together on a few teams that included Corey Allen (UGA WR, '94-'98) and Super Bowl MVP, Hines Ward. The team Twon and I played on with Corey and Hines was called the Morrow Lake City White Sox. There was one team we played for, called The Chico Renfro All-Stars under the leadership of Derrick Stafford, that was life changing for all of us. Derrick is a veteran NBA referee and he exposed us to the finer things in life. His house was huge, his cars were foreign and he kept our uniforms fresh! Derrick's friends list included Michael

Jordan, Charles Barkley and any other notable NBA athletes and personalities you could think of. Once I asked Derrick if he could get me an autograph, he slowly turned to look at me and said, "Stop trying to get autographs and focus on making a name for yourself!" Even though that hurt my feelings a bit, what he said was permanently ingrained in my heart.

When were in the 11th grade, Twon got us a job working as ushers for the Atlanta Braves. One of his coaches was an usher, so Twon went to him and asked about getting jobs for both of us. That's just the kind of person he was; whenever he had an opportunity to come up, he always looked out for me too. I knew that he believed in my ability and my dream of playing professional baseball and getting me this job put me close to major league action on a regular basis. I remember being at Fulton County Stadium when the Braves signed Fred McGriff. It was the same day that a fire broke out in the media booth and I was there – LIVE!

Being an usher for the Braves is a big deal. I took that job very seriously. During orientation and each game day, my supervisor would stress the importance of not allowing fans to stand in the aisles and breezeways. Once during a night game, I had my first experience enforcing this cardinal rule. A gentleman was standing in my breezeway, and I told him, in a polite and professional manner, that he had to move. Even though I was a kid and this was a grown man, I had no hesitation or fear because I didn't want to lose my job and be a bad reflection on Antwon. The gentleman moved just a little, but was still pretty much in my breezeway. He didn't have a rude demeanor towards me, and at the same time, I needed him to get out of my breezeway before my supervisor came over and checked me. Sure enough, I see my supervisor coming over and I'm thinking I'm about to get in trouble. My supervisor smiles at the man and they start talking and laughing. After the man walks off, my supervisor asks me if I knew who that was. I looked dumbfounded I'm sure; I'm a 17-year-old aspiring professional baseball player living the dream of working at a professional baseball stadium; all I was worried about was not losing my job because some dude wouldn't get out of my breezeway when I asked him to. My supervisor laughed and told me the man was Stan Kasten who at the time was the President of the Braves.

Another perk of my job with the Braves was when I would leave from work walking through the area where fans waited for players. If it was dark enough outside, the only thing they could see was the silhouette of someone afar off emerging out of the walkway. In that moment, I was a famous Major League Baseball player until I came into full view and met the fans faces of disappointment of a tall, athletic looking kid who was just an usher. That moment was powerful for me and still stays with me today.

As you read this book, know that I have in no way given all the mentors and influencers in my life the credit they deserve and some I didn't even get to mention. The book would have been way too long. My first pass as an author is to write an introductory work that I hope will inform, inspire and influence others to look at the moments in their lives with a new focus. My valleys are just as important to me as my mountain tops, more so even because I learned how to view disappointments, failures, and times of uncertainty as grit builders that position me to make better decisions later on in life. I learned how to look at the moments in my life that were transformational and trace those moments back to special people in my life. Without Antwon, a lot of my baseball experiences would be erased. I am forever grateful to him for his brotherhood towards me. I hope this book is helpful to you; thanks for taking the time to read it.

Now let's go build some grit...

INTRODUCTION

My name is C.J. Stewart and this is my story of passion, purpose and grit. This is also a story of how I used baseball in Atlanta's inner city to establish L.E.A.D. (Launch, Expose, Advise, Direct), an organization that is aptly named to bring change for the better.

My passion towards inspiring Black youth started at an early age. As a former outfielder in the Chicago Cubs organization, I became a hitting instructor and scout after my playing days. Soon after, I founded the L.E.A.D. organization in 2007 along with my wife, Kelli. Our goal was simple: use baseball to develop strong, youth players who would grow to become successful, responsible adults. L.E.A.D. stands for Launch, Expose, Advise, Direct and my organization does this with young men in some of Atlanta's roughest neighborhoods, who desire to play baseball and become star performers beyond the field.

L.E.A.D. impacts youth baseball in Atlanta by providing comprehensive, year-round programming for middle and high school students in Atlanta Public Schools. Our

1

programming is rigorous and we demand a high level of commitment from our Leaders (middle-school participants) and Ambassadors (high school participants). I believe that by creating an environment of accountability that fosters discipline, we are intentionally molding future game changers in baseball and in life.

I remember in our early years, I was asked a very simple question that I couldn't answer by a board member – 'What are we doing and why does L.E.A.D. exist?' Although I knew in my heart and my head what I was doing through L.E.A.D., I wasn't able to communicate it well to others. Ten years later, I can answer that question with confidence. L.E.A.D. exists because Atlanta won't live up to being a world class City until hundreds of thousands of Black boys can live a sustainable life of significance. My team and I are leveling the playing field in baseball and in life for kids who are often counted out before they step up to bat.

A sustainable life of significance, so what does that mean? What or who does that look like? For me, the development of a complete player would be a combination of Andrew Young and Jason Heyward; former Atlanta mayor and one of Major League Baseball's young superstars. Heyward is a dear friend of mine who started out as a long-time client. I began working with him during his early teens and it's been extremely rewarding to see him mentor and support our Ambassadors over the years. Heyward once told me that he feels L.E.A.D. is necessary because of the opportunities it provides for Black kids to access levels of amateur baseball that put them on a pathway to higher level opportunities. That sentiment I know all too well; if not for kind people in my community connecting me with, and often paying for my access to, high profile, competitive baseball opportunities, I would not have the accomplishments that I do today.

L.E.A.D. is bigger and deeper than baseball. It is the manifestation of the grit the game has taught me and the gift that God has given me to share with others.

CHAPTER 1

Home Plate – Assessment
Birth – Age 10

I am the son of Willie and Bertha Gail Stewart. I was born April 10, 1976 to these very young and determined individuals. My mom was 16 and my dad was 25. I am a 'Grady Baby' and for all intents and purposes that meant that I was Black and poor. Although she was only 16, my mother was very mature for her age. I would later learn that she survived some very unfortunate incidents when she was a child, yet she persevered instead of giving up. I know exactly where I get my spirit of determination from.

Although I've always been told that we lived in Hollywood Courts as a child, I recently learned from my father that we actually lived in Hollywood Brooks which housed Black families that lived at or below the poverty level; a.k.a housing projects. I lived during the era of Wayne Williams, so I was watched closely and played outside with a level of fear that no child should experience. Although I was a black boy living in poverty, my saving graces were being a member of Elizabeth Baptist Church, a student of Atlanta Public Schools and a citizen of Atlanta. My church gave me knowledge about Jesus Christ who I confess is the Son of God and the Savior of the world. Atlanta Public Schools educated legendary Civil Rights leader, Dr. Martin Luther King Jr., Maynard Jackson, who was Atlanta's first Black Mayor and Chick-fil-A founder Truett Cathy who lived in America's first housing project. Being a citizen of Atlanta gave me great pride also because we were the first city in the South to have a Major-League baseball team thanks to the courage of Mr. Bill Bartholomay and 399 other White businessmen from Atlanta. As if that weren't enough, we were and still are the home of Coca-Cola, The Centers for Disease Control (CDC), CNN and Delta. I knew most of these things about my City when I was kid; I couldn't help but feel empowered.

At home, the primal neighborhood cues such as unmanicured lawns, boarded up buildings, drug activity and trash thrown all around proved that I was poor and had a slim chance in hell of making it out. Nevertheless, I had hope. For many parents, television provided an outlet, a vision of what life could be. For my mom, soap operas were her other world. While CJ is my chosen name, my government name as we say around my way, is

6

Corteney James. I got my middle name from my dad, but my first name is after an 'All My Children' soap opera star Palmer Cortlandt. He was a powerful and influential white man who was the founder and owner of Cortlandt Electronics. Soap operas allowed women to dream dreams and my mother had a dream that her baby boy, Corteney, would one day grow up to become a powerful and influential Black man in Atlanta.

At Grove Park Elementary School, I was "that kid" that would come to school with creased khakis, pressed collared shirt and loafers. My mom made sure that I knew who I was to become. Needless to say, that my clothing was different from several of my peers. Not that they were dressed in rags or dirty, but I appeared to be almost presidential every day.

Between Weekly Readers, Sesame Street, Mr. Rogers, my strict teachers and my "uber-attentive to details" mother, I was an exceptional student that was on track to becoming a doctor, lawyer or engineer. This was before I fell in love with baseball at age eight. My grandfather Horace Dunn was a hardworking man who was good to his family, and he enjoyed watching Cubs baseball games; almost always with a Coca-Cola with maybe a lil' something else in it. He was content when he was eating and/or watching Cubs baseball games in the daytime. I would sit with him at his home on Beecher Street and drink a Coke with him (minus the lil' something), and we would sit there watching Andre Dawson with the loud air conditioner in the background hanging out of the window. The vroom of the A/C would compete with the Hotlanta air outside and the voice of Harry Carey coming from the television. It was awesome and I remember saying that baseball was what I wanted to do when I grew up. 'I can do that!' I said to myself.

According to my mom and teachers, playing sports was for fun and being educated was the ticket out of poverty and the only way to be respected as a Black man. It was also the era of "Dumb Jocks". Athletes were considered dumb. The problem was that I didn't want to be an engineer, doctor or lawyer, and so when I made up my mind to play baseball, I felt that I was a let-down. I began to hate school and only performed well out of compliance.

My grit check moment at home plate was around eight years old. My mom and dad would get into verbal fights that mostly ended up with my dad getting kicked out of the house; his clothes being thrown out of our top apartment window into the shrubs. I remember standing there in tears wondering how I could function without my dad. He was a strong and physically statured man that didn't fight back with words or his hands. I get my calm temperament from him and my fiery one from my mom. The cause of the fights? What else? Money and the lack thereof. As I got older, I also sensed that the tension in the household came from my parents' not knowing how to make better lives for themselves and for me and my siblings. Obviously, they didn't grow up saying they wanted to have a family and live in poverty and uncertainty. This environment game me the experience I needed to know that I didn't want that either.

I remember one time my dad was kicked out of the house by my mom and I ran out of the house and got in the car with him. He told me that everything would be alright and that he would be back after a few days. He would always come back and he's always been here. I learned then that he loved my sister Nicole and me enough to fight emotional battles with my mom. He taught me that in life I had to have a strong enough WHY to deal with the stress and unavoidable challenges of life. At that time for me, as an eight-year-old, my unavoidable challenge was being yelled at by a strict mother who had dreams for me that I didn't want.

At age 9, we moved into our first house off Collier Drive. It was still in the inner city of Atlanta, but we were moving on up like the Jeffersons. My parents have always worked hard and would make sacrifices to make sure that we could live the "American Dream" of owning a house. To this day, I don't know if we owned or rented that house, but in my mind, we owned it and that gave me hope. Living in a home versus a housing project made me feel empowered and better than my peers. I remember watching the movie Trading Places starring Eddie Murphy. There was a scene when he was in his new mansion and he came out of the bathroom with a plush robe and an ascot. I immediately made my own ascot using a bath towel and coupled it with my red and royal blue Spider man house robe. You couldn't tell me nothing! The only drawback to the house we lived in was that it made me feel disconnected from my friends. When you're Black, success is a double-edged sword: do too well in something and you could be accused of trying to "act white" and lose your Black card. Even though I have no idea of the logistics surrounding how we got the house, being in it, made me feel better about myself and my circumstances; anything was better than Hollywood Road.

Grit Bit

At the end of each chapter, I'll share a Grit Bit which is simply the main takeaway of what I've shared in a chapter. Grit is what's produced after you've endured a situation in your life that was unexpected and unintended.

I didn't intend to be born into poverty to a teenage, unwed mother and a meagrely educated father, but because I endured that situation and didn't let it define me, it's made me a more driven and determined person.

So here is what I want you to absorb after reading this chapter: I am taking time to take you to my past because I want to show you the importance of having a dream. That dream must be fuelled by passion. My ultimate dream in life was to play for the Cubs. I had troubling and conflicting things happening in my life that I was keenly aware of, and this motivated me to be successful. Your ultimate dream should be something that keeps you working no matter how troubling and conflicting the feedback is in your environment. It's the destination in your life that makes you madly in love with the process of reaching it. Sometimes we are so debilitated by our circumstances that we can't dream. Not having the appetite to dream is a sign that we've done the one thing we never have the luxury of doing – giving up on ourselves.

As you read this book, I want you to think about the things that you dreamed of becoming when you were two, five, eight and ten years old. Don't compare yourself to your peers, rather, compare and contrast your outcomes to your upbringing.

CHAPTER 2

1st base
3K Swing - Age 11-20

At age 11, we moved to College Park - the suburbs. Evidently, there was a time when College Park was predominately white; I never knew that time. To me, College Park was a place where Black folks were moving on up. I was in a neighborhood with several two parent Black families and many had college degrees. My parents didn't have much, but we were there. Lots of hard work, sacrificing and saving money seemed to be finally paying off.

I wasn't excited about making new friends. I had never heard of College Park prior to living there. The first day in the neighborhood I had to stand my ground as I accepted a challenge to fight; a kid named Kendle who was about my age and lived behind us made it known that I would have to fight for any respect I wanted to gain. It wasn't a "hey man, you like sports or do you want to go bike riding?" It was "I wanna fight you and you have to fight me." I came to find out that this was a traditional initiation for all new boys in the neighborhood. I never told my parents about it. It would have crushed them to know that we had moved from the hood to the burbs and this type of stuff was still happening.

As usual, my best friend baseball kept me engaged and busy doing the right things most of the time. I joined a new park for sports called Old National Athletic Association (Old National). I played football and baseball there. I made a lot of good relationships that proved to be very valuable because when I got to Ronald McNair Middle School (McNair), I began to see the guts of College Park from a criminal perspective. By choice, I never sold drugs, stole cars or robbed people, but the opportunity was always there for me if I ever wanted to.

A grit moment for me at McNair was when I skipped school for the first time with a friend I'll call E. He was popular, well dressed, had lots of freedom, but not a sports guy. He set it up for us to go to some girl's house. At this point, I was a student with perfect attendance in school and I ended up graduating high school with perfect attendance as well, so you can imagine my distress when I was approached with this stunt. Even still, knowing that all the teachers and staff knew my parents, and that I would certainly be missed if I left school could not deter me from the possibility of having sex with a girl. Unfortunately, the lure of having sex for the first time was much stronger than my character at that time.

I guess somebody from the school called my house to inform my parents that I wasn't in class. It was one of the most stressful days of my life that ended with me being whipped with a belt, and restricted from television and hanging out with friends. And to add salt to my wounds, the girls wouldn't even have sex with us. I learned at that point that anything that you try to obtain without peace of mind is not worth having.

By the time I left middle school and went to Westlake High School, I was established as a premium athlete who was charismatic and smart. School was a means to an end for me to be drafted by my childhood team – the Chicago Cubs. Baseball was everything to me; I was good at it and I knew it. A defining moment for me in high school happened my sophomore year when I was a backup quarterback on a strong junior varsity team, and the starting shortstop on a below average varsity baseball team. I was flashy and the best on the team (think I mentioned that already). A ground ball was hit to me at short. I fielded it smoothly with plenty of time to throw the runner out at first. I had a strong arm, and so of course,

I took my time and threw him out. (And it still wasn't close.) My head baseball coach, Dave Whitfield, screamed from the dugout "get rid of the ball faster next time!", and I responded with "I got him out, didn't I?!" He immediately ran out to me, got in my face, took my position, made me take off my jersey and told me to go to the locker room. While I was on my way to the locker room, he informed me that I was no longer on the team. For the first time in my life in sports, somebody didn't give me an opportunity to talk my way out of a bad character decision. Safety nets of comfort hinder us from taking responsibility for our negative actions and changing our behavior. My parents and teachers would check my bad attitude and behavior, but most coaches wouldn't because I was always one of the best players on the team. The conflicting messages I received from my coaches, teachers and parents always made me feel like I could talk my way out of trouble. This was not a good thought for a high school kid to have.

My junior year of high school was crazy. I was focused on making money, getting girls, getting drafted and/or a baseball scholarship, getting good grades and church in that order. I was bucking up at my mom and could no longer deal with her strict rules. I had a 9pm phone and bed curfew – as a junior! It annoyed me a lot. I can't remember the amount of "C'mon man! I'm a good kid", I uttered. I had never been arrested, had perfect attendance, B honor roll, was respected by my peers and their parents, and I didn't sell or do drugs. Unfortunately, I felt like I was being treated like a repeat offender at home. It was getting bad. My mom was still trying to whip me with a belt for not washing the dishes, or talking on the phone to my girlfriend after 9pm. As a means of lashing out, I became disrespectful because I was trying to have the freedom that I thought a good kid like me had earned.

My mom had a narrative for my life that was written by All My Children and The Oprah Winfrey Show. During that time, I was listening to N.W.A. and didn't get around to watching much Oprah, so I was on a totally different wavelength. My Mom didn't want me to end up a wayward kid, but she didn't accept that she didn't have the knowledge or experience to put me on track to be a doctor, lawyer or engineer. She grew up in struggle and was angry; she did a great job of keeping me angry too.

I finally made a move. I moved out of the house the summer going into my senior year with my best friend, Eric Hayes, his mom, stepdad and brother. It was peace in their house and I was treated great. We ate a lot because Mr. Gay was an awesome cook and enjoyed cooking. Eric had privileges and we never got in trouble or violated rules because of the mutual respect that we had for his mom, Ms. Gay, who quickly became a second Mom to me. I learned then that respect is a powerful and indivisible tool that bridges dreams to reality. Despite not having my parents in my life full time, I still went to several proms, graduated from high school, signed a Division I scholarship, stayed out of jail, didn't get anyone pregnant and was drafted by the Chicago Cubs. The secret sauce to achieving all those goals was great relationships with people that set boundaries while allowing me space to become who I wanted to be.

I got into Georgia State University at age 18. I wanted to stay in Atlanta because of my girlfriend who I had been with for two years up to that point. I also loved my city. As much as earning a DI scholarship was a dream realized, it was a real nightmare. There I was on campus freshly removed from high school with honors and about to fail out. The stereotype threats were so strong in college. I didn't feel comfortable. There were four Black baseball players on the team including me. Three of them stayed at home while I stayed in student-athlete housing in Buckhead (for crying out loud) with my white teammates.

I fulfilled every stereotype they held about Black people. I was lazy and I still didn't care much for school, not because I couldn't do the work, but because I wanted to play professional baseball. I was drafted out of high school, but opted not to go because my Mom thought I needed to mature. My everyday purpose at State was waiting until I could get drafted again. My plan was to do enough to get by. I was familiar with the mantra of having good study habits, but I never had to have them to get good grades in high school. My good grades there came from being present, behaving and doing my homework.

Even though my grades were tanking from my poor academic work ethic, I still played well on the field, but that wasn't enough to save my scholarship. After an unsuccessful year at GSU, I transferred to DeKalb Junior College for what was supposed to be a less intimidating and intimate environment, but the same thing happened. I didn't go to class, played well on the field and failed out. My issue? At the end of the day I knew that I wanted to play for the Cubs and that's what I should have done when they drafted me out of high school. As it turned out, lighting struck twice for me, and sure enough, at age 20, I was drafted again by the Cubs - this time I signed.

My rookie year was pretty easy, and scarily similar to college except during the time that I would have been skipping classes, we were on the field – all the time! I battled a knee injury that I suffered in college and had surgery, but was not able to fully recover because I didn't take care of myself. Hanging out in clubs and playing video games got most of my attention, so a lot of my days at practice were performed under sleep deprivation. I wish that I had a mentor that would have told me how stupid I was to have my dream come true - to be a Cubbie - only to treat the opportunity like a vacation rather than an occupation.

My coaches didn't know what to do with me. I had talent, but lacked character and grit. People say that things and people get better with time. Come on 21!

Grit Bit

Why all these tales? I had to grow to understand the importance of putting away childish behaviors. No more slaps on the wrist and using charisma to get out of responsibility. I became so distracted by my talent; instead of using it as a platform for opportunity, I used it as a crutch to make up for my slackness. Yet grit is developed through struggle, and boy was I strugglin'!

Talent without grit is uninspiring. No one wants to hear the story of the kid who could do everything and had everything given to him. Talent has the potential to become a distraction when we don't have the right context. During this part of my life, my dreams were being tested by my circumstances; and I was failing miserably.

CHAPTER 3

2nd Base
Diamond Skill Build (Developing skills)
Age 20-30

I got married and became C.J. during this time. At age 20, I was in the minor leagues with the Cubs along with another Courtney. To avoid confusion, he remained as Courtney and I took on the nickname, C.J., for Courteney James Stewart. If you've noticed so far, there has been some variation in how I spell my first name. My mom spelled it Corteney, but somewhere along the line I decided to spell it Courteney. A practice that would drive my soon to be wife crazy.

In addition to dreaming of becoming a Chicago Cub, I also dreamed of being married at age 21. My parents didn't have the model relationship, but they were together and what they did model was a man and a woman sticking life out together, for better or worse. My dream woman would be dark skinned like my mother, full figured and have an amazing smile. I had a vision in my mind of what she looked like, and now all I had to do was find her.

On September 7, 1996, I was home from the regular season with my farm team living with my parents. It wasn't ideal, but Minor League baseball doesn't pay all that well; it's like an internship in Major League Baseball with a modest stipend. I wasn't a franchise baby, so I didn't have a large signing bonus to support me.

On that day, my dad asked me to drive to Atlanta to pick up my younger sister. It was after 9pm and with 30-45 minute drive ahead of me from Stone Mountain, I was aggravated to say the least. About 15 minutes into the ride on I-20, I passed by a pretty dark skinned girl that had the brightest smile. She was on my right side and I signalled for her to pullover, so that I could get her number. She signalled no. I'm not an aggressive guy when it comes to women, and most of my friends at the time may have referred to me as shy; however, I couldn't let her get away, so I followed her off the exit and she pulled into a well-lit gas station where I approached her car. She held some pepper spray to the window of the car and I asked her if she was planning to spray me. She replied by asking me if I would do anything to give her a reason to spray me. Funny, but I got the digits.

On September 15th, I left for winter camp with the Cubs and I returned on October 31st. Knowing that I would soon have to leave for a longer stint for the regular season, I was not about to leave my love for this young lady unknown. One day in March, before I left for Spring Training, I got down on one knee and asked her to marry me. She said yes and on November 23rd the following year, that pretty dark skinned woman with the awesome smile that I dreamed about as a child became my wife. Her name is Kelli Stewart.

I was still the immature Courteney while Kelli and I were married. Kelli was the opposite of me in that she had a strong work ethic. I was still lazy and had an entitlement attitude. I had no college education and would soon no longer be a professional baseball player. At the end of the following season after we were married, I was released by the Chicago Cubs. I returned home to become a full time professional batting coach in East Cobb, GA. It was the best job ever. I got paid $30-$40 per hour to baby sit kids. I didn't know what I was doing as a coach and the parents really didn't care. The fact that I played professional baseball seemed to be enough for everyone and I just rolled with it.

At the age of 25, Kelli and I were pregnant with our first child and I was 4 years in as a professional baseball swing coach. I was having lots of success as a coach and became high in demand to coach travel baseball teams. Ironically, I discovered that I enjoyed coaching more than playing baseball. I wanted to be good as a coach, but I had two problems. The owner of the training facility didn't need me to be great because a lot of money was being made off me just being mediocre. The other problem was that there was no high standard for me to see and emulate in the baseball coaching industry, so I had to set my own. I wanted to dress like the golf pro instructors and have their rates. I wanted to be able to explain and repeat the success that I was having as a coach. I felt that good coaches became great simply by being able to repeat what they do. I lacked and needed a philosophy and methodology that separated me from my peers in the industry. I began to research people and programs online, but couldn't find what I was looking for.

Our first daughter, Kourtni Mackenzi, was born on May 3, 2001, and on the next day, I told Kelli what every new mother wants to hear from her husband – I quit my job. I'm not real sure about censorship standards and such, so I won't tell you what she said. Let's just say, she used a lot of sentence enhancers.

Here I am, 25 years old, with one whole day as a father under my belt, and I quit my comfortable job as a baseball trainer at a well-established training facility. I felt called to start my own company and train clients on my own terms. I was in search of a training methodology that I could call my own, but, in the meantime, I continued to spend hundreds of hours in the batting cage training hitters not really understanding how the training all fit together. One day in 2008, Kelli challenged me to write down everything that I knew about hitting. I had so much fun with it. I had a tape recorder. I was pulling over in the car to write notes. I finally had about 35 pages of bullets and turned it over to my friend and mentor, Bill McLellan, who is Six Sigma certified. The way he processes and simplifies information is surgical. He took all my notes and introduced me to my first training methodology - AT-BATS.

This is what it means:

- Assessment

- Training for strength

- Basics

- Approach

- Training for skill

- Situational hitting

It felt good to know that the frustration I felt about training was summed up in a formula that would allow me to work with clients in a more meaningful way. Now I could discipline myself to do first things first, second thing second and so on. It was a process that I believed in and it worked.

Several weeks before Mackenzi was born, I had a conversation with my good friend and Pittsburgh Pirates pitcher, Kris Benson, and asked him to be Mackenzi's godfather. He said yes. Kelli and I wanted someone that would take care of her if something happened to both of us. A few days before she was born, I got a random call from a guy asking me if I would be home within the hour. I replied yes and he said that I should standby for a delivery. A few hours later, I met the gentleman driving in a new Chevy Tahoe that was loaded. It had two televisions, PlayStation, 12-inch speaker, 20 inch rims, a chrome front grill, wood grain and I was discovering new features on a regular basis. Several months later while I was at home at our apartment relaxing, I went to the balcony of our 2nd floor apartment to use the SUV remote to lock the door. No big deal. Without realizing how, the engine of the SUV started. It was dark outside and I anticipated the worst - that someone was breaking into our truck. We were living in the East Lake community at the time, and although gentrification was well on its way, there were still a few reminders that East Lake Meadows was there. The windows were tinted so I couldn't get a good look inside. The SUV was still parked moments later and I was trying to figure out what was going on. I asked Kris if this had ever happened to him and he laughed and told me that it had a keyless remote. That was my first encounter with a keyless remote and a revelation for my life.

I realized that there are so many things for me to discover about myself that are right in front of me, but I must unlock them. Sometimes unlocking great things comes by accident, like the remote starter, and other times by trial and error. To me, all great things come with a story, so that ultimately God can get the glory.

Around 26 years old, Kelli and I were driving home and she saw a billboard of Michael Vick and said something to the effect that I couldn't play football. To this day, I don't understand why that statement rubbed me the wrong way, but within days, I was seeking professional trainers so that I could develop my body and mind to try out for the Falcons. I hired a speed coach, strength coach, yoga coach, nutritionist and defensive back coach to help me get ready for a workout with the Falcons and Georgia Force. I was never a disciplined athlete in high school, college or the pros. In fact, for one off-season I didn't lift weights, play catch or hit a baseball. I was lazy to the core. I felt that trying to make the Falcons team would help me become disciplined. I thought it would also allow me to reconcile with my failed attempt to be a successful professional baseball player. My diet was strict, and I trained 5-7 days per week for a year. On the day of the workout with the Falcons and Georgia Force I looked like an NFL linebacker and was as fast and as strong. I fell short however in the skill test because I hadn't played in games since high school. I developed so much grit along the way, so it wasn't a waste of time. It was an expensive experiential investment into myself. Without me knowing it, the experience was preparing me to lead in Atlanta. Sometimes you got to be willing to lean into things that seem random to become what God wants you to be.

2006 was a game changer for me. My neighbor from College Park, Maurice Triche, called me out of the blue and asked me if I was still training baseball players. I didn't even know that he knew. I later found out that he was in touch with my parents. He said that he had a school colleague that coached baseball at Stone Mountain High School and was looking for someone to coach his players. I was suspicious because the players were Black and most Black families at that time didn't financially invest into the baseball careers of their sons. I knew this from personal experience.

I had become a narcissistic and disconnected Black man, born and raised in the inner city of Atlanta that was now a successful, professional coach living in the suburbs. As a child, I was always told that I had to get out of the hood and never go back to be successful. It's also what I witnessed other successful people do. And to me, the folks that I did see volunteering their time in poor communities were folks that were forced (court ordered) or incentivized to by their employers.

I didn't know what God was doing in my life by introducing this assignment to me, but I rolled with it.

I allowed the players from Stone Mountain High School to train with me a few times at no cost. It was killing me to do it because I thought that my time was worth money. Through this assignment, I met a family that would later become very supportive and inspirational to the foundation of L.E.A.D. Zabatka "Bat" Walden, Sr. and Bat, Jr. were passionate about baseball. Bat, Sr. began to share his desire for Bat to play college baseball. Bat, Sr. was a single father and didn't have the discretionary funds to invest in travel baseball, private coaching, equipment, travel fees, etc. Although Bat was small in size and I couldn't see him playing at the college level, I wasn't able to tell him that. I grew so attached to him and found myself dreaming about helping him and other Black boys like him – other Black boys who reminded me of me. I worried about him and cried about his plight. I wished that I could somehow save him, but I couldn't because I lacked the funds to do so.

Second base is where I developed my relationship with Christ. I realized that I couldn't make it home without God. I was tired of being the lord of my own life and losing. I was experiencing success based on how I defined it, but wasn't feeling significance and peace of mind.

"Christ-centered possibilities far outweigh man-centered probabilities."

~ Boyd Bailey

Weeks later, one of my most committed clients, who I adopted as my mentor almost from the moment I met him, challenged me by asking me if I was a good hitting coach. Stan Conway has always had swag and confidence; since the first day I met him, I knew he was great at something because of the way he carried himself. So, when he asked me that question, it was time for me to show him a bit of my swag and confidence. I answered the question as if I was a little offended, "Of course I'm a good hitting coach," I replied. In my mind, I'm thinking, "C'mon man!" The next question he asked brought my brain to a screeching halt, "If you're so good, why is it that my son and any kid off the street can have access to you at such a low rate?"

I was stuck. Stan asked me what else I wanted to do with my life, and then I was really stuck. Partially stuck because no one had ever asked me that question before and because my answer was something I didn't know how to make happen. I told him several minutes later that I wanted to start a non-profit organization called L.E.A.D. at the time, I had a few different meanings for the acronym, but hadn't settled on anything. I told him I wanted to become an advocate for black baseball players from the inner city of Atlanta. I wanted to do what was done for me, but on a larger scale and more intentionally. He challenged me to create a budget and get it to him. Of course, I brought Kelli in at this point, because the presentation had to be right. As we were figuring the budget together and the numbers started getting into the tens of thousands, Kelli looked and me with a concerned look and said, "This man ain't gon' give us this kind of money." We finished the budget and reluctantly sent the email to Stan expecting that he would think that I was crazy for asking him for $40,000. He called me a few days later to tell me he had the money and in addition, he had set aside additional funds to invest in a program director. I was like – well damn! I had officially discovered my calling in life and I had the money to get started. This was

2006 and I was age 30. L.E.A.D., Inc. (Launch, Expose, Advise, Direct) became a state recognized non-profit organization in 2007; I was 30 years old and the CEO (Chief Empowerment Officer).

Grit Bit

Are you trying to win at life alone? If so – STOP...NOW! Without my wife bringing stability into my life and without Stan brining focus by asking me tough (and uncomfortable) questions, I don't believe I would be where I am today. Are you trying to win with the wrong team? Winning at the game of life requires that your team be stacked with the right folks. My calling and dreams would have been deferred or derailed if I didn't have the right people in my life. My wife was the best thing that happened to me at this stage of my life. I believe her presence in my life released more favor from Heaven than I could have ever received on my own.

CHAPTER 4

3rd Base
Hitting Lab (Time to Learn New Lessons)
Age 31-40

As I said earlier, having the right folks on your team is essential to winning. Likewise, having the wrong folks on your team can delay and/or jeopardize your wins. As the CEO of L.E.A.D., we've had some bad collaborations and some great ones. The bad collaborations taught me valuable lessons, and positioned me for better relationships down the road. My mentor, Pat Alacqua, taught me the importance of Should Ask Questions (SAQ's) over Frequently Asked Questions (FAQ's) when getting deals done. He also taught me the importance of establishing what must happen and what must not happen on the front end of conversations. I realized from my bad collaborations that I loved L.E.A.D., but I lacked the courage to defend it, even when we were disrespected.

People will do to you what you allow them to do. SAQ's make the conversations go deep. Determining what must and must not happen on the front end of potential collaborations helped me defend L.E.A.D. before I needed to, and It also put people on notice that we weren't messing around.

During this time of learning new lessons, I met the founder of InMotion Air which is a company that sells inflatable batting cages. It's a perfect option over building a stationary batting cage. It inflates in ten minutes and deflates in less than twelve minutes. You can store it in the trunk of most cars, but it takes at least four people to handle it. All in all, it is a great piece of equipment, with a healthy price tag - $12,000. At the time, we needed one for L.E.A.D., but couldn't afford it. Even though it wasn't in our budget at the time, I thought it was a great product and the owners were good people who I wanted to help do well, so I shared the product with others. A good friend of mine, Russell Wrenn, was the head coach of The Westminster Schools at the time and he was looking for a way to maximize and enhance his practices. I told him about InMotion Air, connected him with the owners and he decided to purchase from them. Over the next few years, Coach Wrenn would allow us to borrow one of the 30-foot sectional batting cage for events. Recently we had an event and I asked current coach, Chad Laney, if we could borrow one of the sectionals. He was happy to help, so I reached out to Enterprise Rent-A-Car to rent a pickup truck to transport the cage. I arrived at Enterprise early the morning of our event expecting to pick up a pickup truck and out comes a huge moving truck. I was on a tight schedule and figured that it wasn't worth the hassle to correct the "mistake". I figured that we would simply have more than enough room. I arrived at Westminster to pick up the 30-foot sectional and saw that they actually had three 30 foot sectionals. I asked Coach Laney which one of the three that I should take. He turned to me and said, "Actually we want to donate all three to L.E.A.D. You got something big enough to hold them all?" Remember that moving truck that was supposed to be a pick-up truck? God knew what was on Coach Laney's heart and through the "mistake" at Enterprise, God made sure I readily equipped to receive this blessing.

Forty brought me a lot of joy and some sadness. My grandmother, Lizzie Moss (Grandma Moss), passed on Sunday, August 14th. She endured so much. One of her children lost his life to AIDS, others battled alcoholism, mental illness and homelessness, while others became successful business owners and a tenured employee at a great company. Not to mention all the things she had to endure by being a Black woman growing up during the times of overt racism and discrimination. I remember her once saying to another relative that she would never let her children or anyone else run her to her grave too soon. Everyone else's emergency was not her emergency, and when she felt she had done all she could to help someone, she was done. She was 91 when she transitioned and she went in peace; she wasn't afraid to go to Heaven to see The Lord. I watched her with admiration because she wasn't afraid to die. Grandma Moss taught me how to protect my peace, so that I can genuinely have joy in my life.

Grit Bit

When your calling in life is revealed to you, protect it, defend it. Don't let anyone waive your deficiencies in front of your face and entice you to let down your guard. As in the case with the inflatable cages, God will position you to get what you need when it's time. And whatever you do, protect your peace, so that you can live a joyous life. Living out your calling will present its own fair share of stress, don't let unnecessary things creep into your life that will prevent you from being your best self. Protect your peace.

CHAPTER 5

The Vision

People often ask me what my role is in L.E.A.D. I am the co-founder along with my wife, Kelli. I also double as the visionary and the CEO (Chief Empowerment Officer). My vision kicked off to a blurry start. It took me a while to know what I wanted to do and what I was supposed to do. Clarity didn't come until I met a gentleman named Dez Thornton. Dez gave me a visual story that vividly brings to life what I do.

Imagine a crocodile infested river. On one side, you have zebras trying to cross to get to the food that's on the other side. As the zebras enter the water, some will make it across without incident; others will inevitably get caught and become entangled within the crocs' jaws. Some will die, some will manage to break free yet with many scars. Some of those scars will heal and others may never heal.

The zebra represent Black boys in the inner-city of Atlanta. The crocs represent three evils in life that are designed to destroy them: crime, poverty and racism. I decided to not be a spectator on the side line of this struggle. I am in the crocodile infested river, in a boat, waiting to rescue any young man that will grab hold of the baseball bat that I extend to them. If they choose to grab hold of my bat, I will pull them into my boat and take them across the river safely. I represent a survivor. By being in the boat in the croc infested river, I'm demonstrating to the boys and young men that I understand your circumstances because I've been through it too, and because of God's Grace and Mercy I was able to survive. Confidence is a by-product of survival. It is my duty, my burden and my blessing to provide a safe passage for others.

The media has portrayed Black boys as nuisances in their respective communities. This is the narrative touted in the media and other propagandist outlets. The narrative is that all Black boys – all Black people for that matter- living in America's inner cities are violent criminals. Here in Atlanta, we even have the data to support this faux narrative:

- Many of our inner-city neighborhoods have been rated the most dangerous of America's inner-cities,

- Youth from three Atlanta zip codes – 30310, 30315, and 30318 – grow up to comprise 80% of Georgia's prison population.

- Black boys in Atlanta have about a 40% chance of graduating at all or on time.

When I hear this narrative, I recognize it for what it is – lies! However, do others know that this is false? Are they aware that this is a gross misinterpretation of an entire race? I mean, black people are living better today than we have ever been and this is the only narrative media can come up with. Think about, the rise in meth and heroin use across the nation is triple and even quadrupled in some places, but you don't see that plastered all over the news disparaging white people. In fact, when you do see it, it's a heartfelt tale of how great the white person was before he got on drugs and how he's just sick and needs help. Propaganda is a trip. Black folks who are drug addicts and who resort to crime to fuel their habits are criminals who need to be locked up. White folks, on the other hand, who are drug addicts and resort to crime to fuel their habit should be looked at as sick patients who need help, not incarceration. I digress.

There came a time when I could deny my calling no more. I decided to open my mouth and share my dreams with people who had the influence, power and resources to help them come true. I decided to partner with Atlanta Public Schools (APS) through L.E.A.D. and through the Rotary Club of Atlanta West End. People often ask me, why APS? Even though I graduated from Westlake High School in Fulton County, my foundation years as a young boy and young man were in APS; even before I was born. The first time I was inside an APS school was when my mother was pregnant with me. She started off at Doug, but when she got pregnant, she had to go to night school at Washington to finish her education. I was born at Grady Hospital and during my early years, we lived in Hollywood Brooks. My mom also received some educational and career support from The Job Corps, right on Westlake Avenue. Ironically, when I was a little boy in the day care at Job Corps, I had no idea that one of the ladies who I saw everyday, Ms. Florene Hutchings, was the aunt of my wife who I would meet some 17 years later.

My life has been orchestrated so well by the Lord. I say that as a reflective statement and as a faith statement. Some people have called me a celebrity, and at times I must check my ego because what kid from the hood doesn't want to be a celebrity? If being a celebrity helps me get more black boys across that crocodile infested river, then I'll be that; but being a celebrity to me is the personified in touchable people we see in our lives everyday – not the untouchable ones. I am just like most of you reading this book. I was on Food Stamps (and I'm talking about when you had the food stamp book with actual stamps), TANF, Medicaid and WIC; all those daily tell-tale reminders that you were born at the bottom and you have absolutely no shot of making it out of the gutter. Sadly, some 40 years later that sentiment still rings true. A child born into poverty in Atlanta today has about a 4% change of making it out. I have no idea what this stat was when I was a kid; feel like it might have been a 0% chance. Being born into poverty, to a teenage mom and young father should have been a death sentence for me, but I decided I'd do everything to not let poverty get the best of me.

Grit Bit

Grit can be defined as strength of character. This is not based on talent. It is about getting difficult things done even when you don't have the knowledge and resources to do it. Grit is about possessing passion and perseverance. Your passion is found in your suffering. Pinpoint what makes you passionate to the point of madness and therein lies your life's mission. My parents had tremendous grit. To overcome all the uncertainty, instability and stress that poverty imposes on your life and come out on the other end as overcomers takes tremendous grit, indeed.

So why should you feel confident when approaching life's challenges? Because you are approaching life's challenges which means you're still alive and you're in the fight – you're not dead. In fact, the evidence of your grit is that most people would have been destroyed already if they had to grow through what you've been through – and yet, you're still standing (can I get an Amen!) You are a warrior. You are a survivor.

The world has a lot of problems and we need you to believe that you can solve them. You certainly can't solve them all, yet surely you can solve at least one. The world needs you because your grit allows you to get difficult things done and not quit when things get tough.

Embrace adversity, run to it and then conquer it like only you can.

CHAPTER 6

Discover Your Life's Purpose

My parents and teachers began preparing me for college at age five. You probably know that from reading my story in the preceding chapters. College was supposed to be my great escape from poverty. However, the more my loved ones pushed me to become a doctor or lawyer (basically stuff they thought would liberate me from poverty), the more I hated school.

Some of you can relate to this. Even at that age, I knew I was born to serve a higher purpose. All I needed to do was make others around me see it. If you were to ask your closest friends or family members what you are passionate about, they might have no idea. Frankly, I wouldn't blame them. The society we live in is wired this way. Most schools don't teach a class called 'Finding Your Purpose' and therefore it is up to you to discover it.

I discovered my purpose at eight. I'll never forget the moment it hit me: I was eight years old sitting on the couch next to my grandfather, Horace Dunn, watching a Cubs baseball game. My grandfather loved his family, loved a good meal, loved his spirits and he loved baseball. As we sat there straining to hear the voice of Cubs' announcer Harry Carey over the roaring A/C in the window, Andre Dawson swung at an 0/2 pitch and sent the ball sailing off the edge of the TV screen for a 3-run homer. I remember saying, "that's what I want to do when I grow up!" From that moment (this happened more than thirty years ago) till this one - it has been crystal clear that my destiny was tied to baseball.

There is something both magical and maddening about discovering your life's purpose at an early age. On the magical side, think child prodigy like Michael Jackson or Mozart; you've been blessed to find your thing early in life which will afford you more time to perfect it. On the maddening side, being a Black inner-city kid presented all kinds of reminders that I was too poor to even afford the dreams of playing professional baseball. The everyday signs - unattended landscaping, graffiti, trash build-up, abandoned homes, etc. – reminded me of the uphill journey to simple success, let alone achieving something as gargantuan as playing pro ball.

Despite my circumstances, I was filled with hope. My hope turned into ambition and my ambition eventually turned into GRIT, which I define as the relentless pursuit of purpose. This turned out to be my First Base line curiosity statement: Now, if you're anything like me, you're probably wondering why you should continue reading this book. That's completely fair. I'll give you two reasons:

- You could have been doing other things, but you are reading this now and you have come this far. It's no accident that you got this book or that someone gave it to you to read.

- I've spent my entire life mastering mistakes and adapting to change. My story may not be exactly like yours, but adversity is no respecter of person; you can relate to something in my testimony. I've gathered my tears, fears, frustrations and triumphs and packaged them into a proven process that not only guarantees home runs in baseball, but will guarantee home runs in life as well. And everybody wants to hit a few out of the park, right?

By systematically sharing my story of struggle and success, I hope to inspire you to give yourself permission to take focused action on a progressive business goal or build stronger relationships in your life – whatever your priority goals may be. I'm going to walk you through a simple, but effective, three step process similar to the one I use to coach amateur and professional hitters.

Grit Bit

Your life's purpose is rooted in your adversity, in your struggle, in things that make you laugh and in things that make you cry. The grit I developed by growing up in poverty has provided me a strong foundation on which to learn, struggle and grow.

Once you've been convicted of your purpose- protect it. Pray for discernment which, to me, is one of those tricky gifts that often doesn't come with empirical evidence. Sometimes, it's the nagging voice in your subconscious mind or that uncomfortable feeling in your gut. Learn to listen and trust this voice. In my life experience, I've found that this feeling was the Holy Spirit speaking to me, and guiding me; even before I was even thinking about being a follower of Christ.

Lastly, use your purpose to make your life and the lives of others better. Poor people are often taken advantage of because it's assumed that they don't know better and can't do better. I've lived under that condescending glare before and it's enough to make you holler and throw up both your hands, as Marvin Gaye said. Protect the poor. You can do this; we must do this. As you and I progress in life and become financially secure, we must not forget the poor.

CHAPTER 7

Discover Your Master Within

The first step to greatness is discovering your master within. These key things are necessary:

- What are you made of?

- How do you press through change? How do you move from failure to success?

- How do you leave an indelible mark?

The school of hard knocks has taught me that we must appreciate our past in order to achieve future success. Therefore, the first step in the process is discovering your master within. This reflective step is designed to help you objectively assess your past, so that you can detect the patterns & habits that got you to where you are today.

The purpose of discovering your master within is to reveal how you are uniquely equipped to take advantage of opportunities and adapt to threats. Think about your life in three phases:

- Age 10 – 20: Deep observation stage.

- Age 21-30: Experimentation stage

- Ages 31- through your current age: Adaptation stage.

As we go back in your past and explore each of these phases, it will ultimately lead us to your master within. I'll use my life as the example to guide you through the process, and I encourage you to examine your own in order to get the most out of this experience.

Let's begin by exploring the **Deep Observation Stage** (10-20). Think back to that decade of your life or if you fall into this age range presently, examine the present life you are living. For most of us, it was the end of elementary school through early adulthood. This decade of our lives is usually made up of a large volume of low quality inputs resulting in a large volume of low quality results. This is the stage where my mom, grandmothers and aunts would say a child is 'smelling himself'; meaning the child thinks he knows everything and is acting without wisdom. While this sounds like a really bad phase, it's actually where the foundation of your grit is formed if you know how to reflect on your experiences in the proper framework.

A Grit Bit moment from my Deep Observation phase occurred when I was around 15 or 16 years old. I learned a hard lesson: there was more to life than baseball. Giving and learning how to earn respect was what I needed to be most concerned about. One incident made it abundantly clear that in order to bridge the gap between my dreams and my reality, I had to learn to respect others and build better relationships.

Remember the experience I shared earlier, when my coach kicked me off the baseball team for my lackadaisical behavior? For the first time in my sports life, an authority figure refused to let me talk my way out of a bad character decision. And remember my example from my rookie year with the Chicago Cubs? It was pretty easy until a knee injury that I suffered in college resurfaced. I ended up having surgery and was not able to fully recover because I didn't take better care of myself. I made the stupid choice of playing video games and hanging out in clubs over getting the proper rest and rehab for recovery. While I was fortunate enough to have my one in a million-dream come true, I squandered it by treating my occupation like a vacation. Once again, that void of character came back to haunt me. Sticking out my chest and making high volume, low quality inputs cost me everything! (Or so I thought.) I'm sure we can all think of an incident from our teens or 20s we wish we could do over. My hope is that you can learn from my mistakes.

Stage Two is called the **Experimentation Stage** (21- 30). As I approached this phase, there was one thing that I was sure of: I wanted to be married at 21. At this stage, it is more about being impressed upon. By this stage, hopefully you've had people in your life who've allowed you to fail, to feel the embarrassment of disappointment and the humility of taking responsibility for your mistakes and your purposeful misconduct. If not, your Deep Observation phase of high volume, low quality inputs that yield low quality results will haunt you for an unnecessary extended period of time. If you've not had these important experiences by the Experimentation State, you're probably used to hearing people tell you things like, 'It's time for you to grow up already,' and 'Why you so childish?'

My Experimentation Stage was a tough decade where I struggled with failure and responsibility. When I met Kelli, this stage became harder and easier at the same time. Harder because I now had the responsibility of being her husband and easier because she set clear boundaries for me on what she was going to tolerate and what she wasn't.

In the early years of our marriage, I was still very immature. Fortunately, Kelli was the opposite. Here I was with no college education and soon to be released by the Cubs and to her credit, Kelli saw something in me that I couldn't see in myself. She patiently etched and chiselled out my sense of entitlement and helped me become the man God wanted me to be all along. Getting married during The Experimentation Phase is very risky. This phase is about taking the foolish things you did in the Observation Phase (because you were smellin' yourself) and turning them into a positive. Hopefully by now, the stubbornness of youth has worn off and you know how to do things like ask for help, be more patient and less impulsive and know when and how to apologize. All of these skills are necessary in order to have a harmonious marriage. Unfortunately, I had none of these skills when I got married and that resulted in a very turbulent first year for Kelli and I (that's a whole other book by itself). I was determined to make our marriage work, however, because in all the uncertain times I witnessed my mom and dad go through as a child – those times never tore them a part. Dating and being married to Kelli forced me to learn how to build relationships, how to keep your word, how to apologize when you fall short and how to focus on self rather than others in order to maintain healthy relationships. I was forced to figure out life beyond baseball, beyond playing baseball rather, and it was extremely uncomfortable.

The valuable lesson I learned during this stage is that I could no longer be lord over my own life. Remember those high volume, low quality inputs? Well the result of all my stubbornness and stupidity was that I was losing, and I was tired of losing. Peace of mind eluded me until I finally surrendered my life to Christ. I realized that I was nothing without Him and my wife. One of my go to bible verses is Matthew 19:26 KJV "But Jesus beheld them, and said unto them: with men, this is impossible; but with God all things are possible." It reminds me that I don't always have to be in control. This is the perfect place to think about a turning point in your life, your calling or your business. What would it be like to reinvent yourself? What would it be like to push your business beyond what you think is possible? Are you willing to face the unknown? Are you willing to adapt?

The **Adaptation Stage** starts from age 31 and continues for the rest of your life. By the time we reach our early 30's we should be able to avoid the wear and tear of our past mistakes by making high quality decisions. As you might imagine, transitioning from being drafted by the Chicago Cubs to being forced out of the game due to injury was a huge, painful and somewhat embarrassing adaptation. Despite all odds, Grit wouldn't let me give up on my eight-year-old self; the boy who saw his entire life through the lens of baseball. No matter what happened next, one thing was sure: my life would continue to revolve around baseball. The only problem was I had no idea HOW. The uncertainty initially caused me great anxiety. After putting myself through severe mental anguish, I had no choice but to step back and focus on the small things that I could control and accept the things I couldn't. Suddenly, I was comfortable being uncomfortable, and miraculously, opportunities began to present themselves. I became a full time professional hitting coach working with students from affluent families, and although I felt like a high-priced baby sitter, I was doing what I loved and providing for my family. It was the best job ever! At first, I had no idea what I was doing, but the parents really didn't care. The fact that I had played professional baseball was enough for them.

The year 2006 was a game changing year for me. It started with an unexpected phone call from my childhood mentor Maurice. He called to ask if I was still training baseball players. We hadn't spoken in quite a while and I didn't even know he knew I was training baseball players. He went on to tell me about a coach at Stone Mountain High School who was looking for someone to coach his players. I was immediately suspicious because I was familiar with Stone Mountain High School and they didn't have a reputation for investing in their players. Despite my hesitation (and with some encouragement from my wife), I allowed the Stone Mountain players to train with me a few times at no cost. I ended up falling in love with an under-sized, scrappy young man named Zabatka (Bat)

Walden, Jr. He and his father would do almost anything for Bat to play college baseball, but they simply didn't have discretionary funds to pay for private coaching and the travel expenses needed for Bat to have a chance. That sounded like an all too familiar story to me. But for the people that God put in my pathway, I would not have been able to take baseball as far as I did.

I strongly believe you find your calling in life based on what you dream about, worry about and cry about. I dreamed, worried and cried about finding a way to open doors for young men who were guilty of the same crime I committed as a child: dreaming beyond your family's resources. I call it a crime because it could have turned into my life sentence of resentment if God had not sent people like Antwon Smith, my God-brother Eric Gay and his mom Ms. Gay and TJ Wilson into my life. They along with others made it possible for me to say, 'I'm a former professional baseball player.' I had officially discovered my calling and had the money to get started.

Grit Bit

In order to be successful, you must have the faith to act before you think you are ready. I'm not talking about arrogance or winging it. I'm talking about that decision we all must make to trust ourselves in unchartered waters. Focus on controlling the small things that you can control.

There's no way I could have predicted Stan investing $40 thousand into my vision. I was diligent in the little things (getting my character together, surrounding myself with good people who could hold me accountable, etc.) and doing those things made Stan feel confident about investing in my vision (and I'm no fool, I know Kelli had a lot to do with his decision as well.)

In a series of events, I moved from single man to a husband of a beautiful wife (and later father). I also moved from being released by the Cubs to uncertain and confused and then professional hitting coach. In a few years, I moved to CEO of a for-profit and non-profit organization to entrepreneur. Since birth, my life has been filled with grit bits that demanded me to adapt to change. Nevertheless, this is not about me. This book is about you. What opportunities are sitting on your tee right now, ready for you to take your best swing? What is possible for your life and business if you simply accepted the fact that you will never be completely comfortable with the unknown? One of my mentors told me, "One of the things you have to get is going!" as it pertains to planning and executing projects. It's easy, safe and comfortable to spend most of your life planning on doing something rather than making the decision to do. Give yourself permission to take that first step.

Discovering your master within focuses on analyzing your past in a bid to maximize your future. Hopefully, these stages will give you a deeper appreciation of how you got where you are today. It will also provoke you to think courageously about how to improve your current condition to get to a more favourable tomorrow.

CHAPTER 8

Pressing Through Change

Pressing through change is where we'll focus on the present. To accomplish this, we're going to approach it the only way I know how to – within the context of baseball. If you haven't played baseball before or you do not know the rules, that's fine, the concepts are very easy to pick up. We are going to use a business organization analogy to set the stage for this exercise. The first group we'll focus on are the owners. Owners represent the catchers on the team, and just like baseball catchers, they facilitate the game. They not only signal what pitches to throw — they are solely responsible for protecting home plate, and making sure that nothing gets by them.

The next group in the organization we'll focus on are the sales people. Sales people are naturally pitchers. Have you ever seen a salesperson in action? They just keep pitching ideas till you have no choice, but to pick one. Just like baseball pitchers, people in sales are usually the flashiest, most visible people in the company who are tasked with pitching a company's products and services.

So far, we have owners (e.g. catchers) who are running the show on the field and pitchers (sales people), who have the most autonomy in the organization because they must sell (pitch) the company's products/services, but where is your pipeline? Here is where we meet the batters, who in a business analogy like this, we'll call apprentices. You're probably thinking, why is an apprentice being put in a role with such high expectation and stress? Let me explain why the apprentice is the perfect batter:

- They usually have no idea what's coming at them, so they must be on the lookout for everything

- They are eager to get a hit to prove themselves worthy.

As a professional swing coach, I take all my clients, through the same process (methodology), and customize the components to fit their situations. Instead of the game of baseball being the focus of this illustration, we'll focus on the game of life. To give you a preview, here are the four steps in the process:

- Assessment

- 3K Swings

- Skill Building

- The Hitting Lab

Think of each step as a position in your life.

Keeping our theme of **Pressing Through Change** and dealing with the present, the first step in your life is Assessment (home plate). The Assessment Phase is designed to put you through simple and complex drills — to see how you respond under stressful conditions. The purpose is to highlight your strengths and expose your weaknesses.

Translate this Assessment to your calling/purpose in life. Think back to various drills you encountered in your childhood. The memories you have that have shaped how you view relationships, how you handle conflict, how you deal with regret. Think about how these drills have affected your romantic and marital relationships, how they've affected your relationship with your kids. And that last point is where I want to focus in this **Assessment Phase**. This reflection is just as much about your children, mentees, siblings as it is about you. Even during the **Assessment Phase**, I believe it's important to keep those who will use your life as an example in the forefront of the process. Doing this keeps us in check and reminds us that we owe future generations an example worth following.

Moving on to **3K Swings** (1st base), this step is all about the numbers. Using the wisdom you've gained from analyzing the **Assessment Phase** of my methodology, it's now time for you to take some risks and get some reps in the game of life. Most baseball players will say you can never get enough reps at your position. To translate that to life, reps equal risks. It would be a damn shame to go through the painstaking process of self-reflection to gather wisdom during the **Assessment Phase**, only to never put that wisdom to the test. Oh, the word 'risk' scares you? Trust me, I understand, but the Grit Bit here is that risk only becomes less scary through repetition. The more you swing at 95 mph fastballs, the better you'll get at loading and approaching that ball. Likewise, the more risk you take to sign up for leadership positions at school, work, church and in your community, the better you'll get at leading others. If success is your aim, repetition/risk is unavoidable and so is failure. Yeah, I said, the 'F' word. Failure is an unavoidable component of success. That's why I said earlier in this book, if you've grown up around adults who've allowed you to experience failure, you'll be so far ahead of the game as you get older. The Grit Bit at this juncture: Abandon the pursuit of perfection and focus on repetition. Done properly those weak areas that were exposed in the assessment will begin to get stronger and new skills will emerge.

Second Base: Skill Building.

Here, the focus is not so much on fundamentals, but the bigger picture; a focus on the concepts that influence your present and eventually your future. At this stage in the methodology you're asking questions like, how do I use my calling in life to provide stability and security for myself, my family, my company, etc. You're asking these types of questions because at this point there should be some evidence of your skill at your calling. What kind of feedback is your life giving you relative to your skill level? Are you experiencing success in the area of your calling? Do you need to increase your risks/reps in order to get more proficient in a certain area? I love the skill building phase because it's not all about fastballs— you also must hit curve balls and sliders. The key to success here is a mix of precision and adaptation.

Third Base: Transition - Hitting Lab.

At this base the final objective is the **Hitting Lab** where you continually sharpen your acumen while thinking about your legacy. How will you share what you've learned with others who want to do what you do? How do you effectively mentor the next generation of you? Ask yourself if you are in the game of life just to cross the finish line, or to leave a legacy.

Grit Bit

The final Grit Bit I'll leave you with outlines the guardrails of my life. Winning at the game of life is a mentally, physically, emotionally, spiritually and psychologically taxing endeavour; but it can be fun if you have the right people on your bus. My core values are the guardrails for my life. They help me determine who gets on my bus and who gets kicked off. My guiding core values are:

- Excellence - fulfilling expectations
- Humility - thinking of yourself less so that you can serve others more
- Integrity - doing the right thing even when you can do the wrong thing
- Loyalty - doing the right thing for the right reasons, even if they're not popular.
- Stewardship - protector of your values and people
- Teamwork - being your best within a group of people that are being their best for a specific purpose

I define them because everybody's definition for excellence may not be the same as mine. And it's important to note that these core values don't make me perfect, however, they make me a more disciplined and accountable human being.

CONCLUSION

Atlanta is regarded as a world class city and I'm confused on how that can be. Children born into poverty have about a 4% chance of making it out and over half of Black boys in Atlanta don't graduate from high school at all or on time. With stats like this (and trust there are many more), being a world class city is the last thing we need to be claiming right now. To me, L.E.A.D. exists because Atlanta can't truly be considered a world class city until hundreds of thousands of Black males experience sustainable lives of significance. Significance is greater than success.

What does living a life of significance look like for Black males in a world class city?

It looks like:

- on-time graduation,
- authentic, consistent investment into youth development programming that has a resolute focus on prevention versus rehabilitation, and

- year-round core value training in our schools as a required school course and via sports programs.

Right now, we have a cradle to prison/grave pipeline; when we have a cradle to CEO pipeline, then talk to me about Atlanta being a world class city.

Don't get me wrong, we are experiencing significant economic growth and expansion, and that's good. But let us not forget that we are also a City whose children are dying right before our very eyes, every day while we cut ribbons and welcome new companies to our communities. A lot of those ribbon cuttings are happening a stone's throw from all the action. All this is happening on our watch.

And that is really sad.

If you want to do something about this and make sure that all economic growth, expansion and revitalization is indeed good for ALL of Atlanta's citizenry, then join me. We are empowering a generation of Black boys who will grow up to become an electorate that is responsible, civically engaged, knowledgeable and gainfully employed. And we need your help to do this great work.

Farmers don't plow and plant without expecting a harvest, and even deeper, farmers don't plow and plant where they don't expect a harvest can grow. Atlanta is fertile with young Black men who can defy the odds that are stacked against them when they're given the right resources. I've used my pain, which has come from my passion, to be a resource; and you can do the same if you're willing to take the risk and execute the methodology I've outlined in this book. You must be willing to be vulnerable, transparent and honest with the person you can lie to the best – yourself. I told myself many lies until I was convicted and accepted the burden and blessing that God has laid on my heart: To empower an at-risk generation to lead and transform the City of Atlanta.

Final Grit Bit

I was at a workshop and heard a speaker say that passion is derived from the Latin root pati-, meaning suffering, or enduring. At that moment, it all made sense to me. The endless amount of effort that I've been willing to invest into my calling has come from the suffering I've experienced over my life and the suffering I see Black boys and young men experiencing now. Kelli always says that the main requirement for doing what we do is that you must be crazy. Considering the fact that the world looks to non-profits to save the world with ten cents, I can understand where she's coming from. We just need to add suffering to the list, too. So, my last Grit Bit is this: Don't run from your struggles in life. These encounters supply the fuel/passion you need to develop the grit that is necessary to relentlessly pursue your purpose in life.

Thank you for taking the time to read this book.

Made in the USA
Columbia, SC
24 November 2019

83766148R00048